BEST 50 POETRIES

HARSH KUDESIA

Contents

Contents

Contents

1. Life

There's a weird thing about life
you always can't hold the
same importance in someone's life.
And i guess,it's totally fine.
In a relationship it's the journey
which matters a lot more then
the final destination.
When a relationship ends it
does bring pain but it's not
always have to be ugly.
Sometimes you can just cherish
the memories you shared with
them and preserve it in the
safest corner of your heart
until you feel like it.
- Harsh Kudesia

2. Life

Love,Like,and be a Friend
to someone who makes
you believe that you
are worth of something.
But don't believe that
Liking by someone
Loving by someone
and becoming a Friend someone
don't makes you Worthy.
Be worthy to yourself,
be worthy of everything
that happens to you in life.
Live a Life with Good Values.
- Harsh Kudesia

3. Life

I have come to
leave one life to
make another life,
I don't know sir,
What have i come to
take in this unknown city,
leaving my Mother.
- Harsh Kudesia

4. Moments

Each time
I click a selfie,
I ensure that
I always wear a Smile.
Those pics are the one
I go back to when i am low.
And that one smile of mine
reminds me what I am capable of.
- Harsh Kudesia

5. Moments

Class is not a
success thing
rather a blend of vision,
progressive thought process,
a strong zeal,a brave heart,
a desire to keep learning
and working hard and
humbleness !!
- Harsh Kudesia

6. Friendship

There is nothing
last forever...
even a darkest night
have beautiful morning !!
So believe me,
your deepest sorrow
have joyful
Tomorrow !!
- Harsh Kudesia

7. Friendship

I have lot's of suggestion but
I always need your final suggestion.
It is easy to make lots of Friends
but i just need your Friendship.
Because i believe in Quality,
Not in Quantity.
And,I don't want to sacrifice
My love and care on a Selfish World.
Because i have the most precious gift
from God and it's you my Best Friend.
- Harsh Kudesia

8. Love

Those who lose hope,
Then there are no
Complaints from them,
I buried my wishes,
now...
I have no requests,
from them !!
- Harsh Kudesia

9. Mother

Mother,you have
bought me,
from every trouble.
Mother my world
is made of you...
Only you are my paradise...
You are my only Wish.
- Harsh Kudesia

10. Life

There are only
two things to worry
about in life:
Either you're free
or you're not.
If you're free,
there's nothing to worry about.
If you're not,
you kick the shit
out of everything
around you until you are.

11. Feelings

Sometimes I feel
like killing my self
when you compare me...
from others
for silly things.
I thought of
not caring but
it's sucks.

12. Motivation

Being grateful
for all...
that you have
and all...
that is yet
to come will
transform the
quality of...
your Life.

13. Motivation

The whole world
bowed down
before you...
never ask for
such a prayer...
but no power in
the world can
bow down to you
definetely ask for this Prayer.
- Harsh Kudesia

14. Love

Most of the
love relationship
fail because one
person gives
priority...
to his/her partner,
and the opposite
person always
tries for better
Option !!

15. Love

The journey is as
far as you are,
the eyes is there
as fas as you are,
I have seen thousands
of flowers in this
gulshan, but the
fragrance is there
as far as you are.

16. Love

Before loving others,
learn to love yourself.
Your soul sitting
inside you is your
first responsibility,
if something happens
to you,
then your god will
also feel pain.
When you start
understanding yourself,
you will understand
the pain of others better.

17. Emotion

The Only Emotion
Yes,you may dwell
into the circus
of lust.
Your firefly will
still sparkle
your way
because it only
knows trust.

18. Life

Remember,one thing
friends win courage in
life...
not a weapon.
There is nothing,
there is no sorrow,
every one has
become helpless...
moonlight is with you,
so what am i missing
is the light,
I am getting from
the darkness.

19. Life

No wish to live,
no wish to die.
Like a living corpse,
now this condition of mine.
Neither the happiness of
anything,nor the sorrow
of anything,
we are living alone
like this.
Million explained to the heart,
in this it is your loss,
here there is no one's identity.
But this heart is ignorant,
I don't know what it is,
I am upset,this alone today.
He cries,but does not say
anything to anyone,not
knowing what he is
stubborn about.

20. Sad

The story of this
heart is also very strange,
it finds...
happiness with great difficulty,
it does not feel
happy when someone
comes near, but it hurts
a lot when it goes away.

21. Motivational

Always have eyes
that see the best,
a heart that
forgives...
the worst,
a mind that
forgets the bad,
and a soul that
never loses hope.

22. Motivational

Close the door to
the past,
open the door
to the future,
take a deep
breath,
step through
and start
a new chapter
in your life.

23. Motivational

There are many
victories left,
many defeats left,
the essence of life remains.
We have gone from
here to the new
destination,
it was only a page,
now the entire book is left.

24. Motivational

Always be yourself.
At the end of the day,
that's all you've really got,
when you strip
everything down, that's
all you've got,
so always be your self.

25. Motivational

Throughout Life
People will make you mad,
disrespect you and treat
you bad.
Let god deal
with the things
they do,
cause hate in
your heart...
will consume you too.

26. Friendship

Fake friends are
those who try
to hide you from
their real life.
Your true friends
will never be
ashamed of you
in public,they
always want to
be seen with you.

27. Friendship

A friend is
someone who
helps you up
when you're
down,and if
they can't they
lay down
beside you and listen.

28. Friendship

True friendship
multiplies the good
in life and divides
it's evils.
Strive to have
friends,for life
without friends
is like life on a
desert island.

29. Love

For every day,
I miss you.
For every hour,
I need you.
For every minute,
I feel you.
For every second,
I want you.
Forever,
I love you.

30. Love

Love is just too
weak of a word
to express,
what i feel for you.
One life is
just not enough
to tell you
how madly in love
i am with you.

31. Love

To love
without condition,
to talk without intention,
to give without reason,
to care without
expectation,
that's the spirit
of true love !

32. Inspiring

The older you get,
the more fragile
you understand
life to be.
I think that's
good motivation
for getting out
of bed...
joyfully each day.

33. Inspiring

Selfishness is not
only taking from
others...
for own success,
but also being
neutral and not
having sympathy
or empathy for others.

34. Inspiring

In lifee there is a
deadline and endurance
limit for everything.
When you wait for
something good to happen,
and it does not,
and the limit is over,
you breakdown.
When good continues and
crosses the deadline,
it becomes toxic.
When you are waiting
for someone,it don't come
you start your saga.
When you wait to hear
from someone and they don't,
you forget them !

35. Inspiring

People don't move
on because they are
hoping that one they
will get return on
investment,
for their emotions.
But my dear it's
not a business deal
it's about soul and
thus no return will come.

36. Inspiring

Accepting or rejecting
somebody's feelings...
is a personal choice but
not acknowledging
someone's feelings is
a bad thing.
Its even worse than
leaving someone
hanging in between.

37. Inspiring

Every morning
you have two
choices: continue
to sleep with
your dreams,
or wake up and
chase them !

38. Inspiring

Actually, we are never
in control of any situation.
We are just puppets playing
our roles.
So, just let certain
things go and allow your
heart to see everything that
is happening as a beautiful
experience necessary to live
through this life.

39. Inspiring

Your vision and
your self -
willingness are the
most powerful...
elements to
conquer your goal.

40. Parents

Two person's are the
most important in this
world that's my
Mom and Dad,
to whom i owe everything
all that i have...
The sun rises from the east
and sets towards west,
no matters what happens
my Mom & Dad are the best.

41. Motivational

Whenever you face
a challenge...
don't ask why me
because, God only
give challenges to
those who are capable
of achieving something.

42. Motivational

Never stop working
for your vision
because you never
know when your
early morning
struggle will
turn into an
overnight success.

43. Motivational

You never change
your life...
until you step
out of your
comfort zone,
change begins at
the end of your
comfort zone.

44. Motivational

Don't dwell on the past.
Your history can't be erased,
but your future has yet to
be written.
Make the most of
what's going to happen
instead of worrying about
what you can't change.
Don't waste your time being
sad,because you're wasting
away moments in which
you could be happy.

45. Thought

A good idea will
keep you awake
during the morning,
but a great idea
will keep you awake
during the night.

46. Inspiring

"YOU CAN CHANGE ..."

You can be a little better.
You can stand a little taller.
You can love a little deeper.
You can pick a different path.
You can walk a different walk.
You can find forgiveness,and joy.
You can become your best you.
Because he gave us life,
you can change yours !

47. Inspiring

You will never
change your life
until you change
something...
you do daily.
The secret of your
success is found
in your daily
routine !

48. Inspiring

Be grateful and give back.
Forgive and move on.
Actively pursue your dreams.
Make a change...
Finish what you start !

49. Inspiring

Success is not a accident,
it is a hard work,
preseverance,
learning,studying,
sacrifice and most
of all,love of
what you are doing

50. Discover

When you are
alone,
you will discover
the rhythm of
your heartbeat.
And realize that
little things are
what matter most.

ABOUT BOOK:

In this book you will get a best poetries... Related to Inspiring,Motivational,Thoughts,Feelings,Love,Life,Etc.

ABOUT AUTHOR:

Harsh Kudesia,has been writing professionally in various capacities for the better part of the last decade.

More About us:

Professionally - Student and Web developer.

Belongs from - Agra,Uttar Pradesh

9 798887 837987

Printed by Libri Plureos GmbH in Hamburg,
Germany